green girl

Jessie Sobey

Nine Mile Books

Publisher: Nine Mile Art Corp.

Editors: Bob Herz, Stephen Kuusisto, Andrea Scarpino

Art Editor Emeritus: Whitney Daniels

Cover Art: "Liquor Peter & Jan," courtesy of the Collection of Christopher B. Steiner

Nine Mile Books is an imprint of Nine Mile Art Corp

The publishers gratefully acknowledge support of the New York State Council on the Arts with the support of the Governor and the New York State Legislature. We also acknowledge support of the County of Onondaga and CNY Arts through the Tier Three Project Support Grant Program. We have also received significant support from the Central New York Community Foundation. This publication would not have been possible without the generous support of these groups. We are very grateful to them all.

Copyright 2021 by Jessie Sobey

ISBN: 978-1-7354463-9-4

with great love & respect
to my *full fathom five*:

Deborah Tall, David Weiss, Jim Crenner,
Melanie Conroy-Goldman, Jasper Bernes

Affection, puh! You speak like a green girl,
Unsifted in such perilous circumstance.
Do you believe his 'tenders,' as you call them?
—*Hamlet*

TABLE OF CONTENTS

Author's Note 9

green girls

Who's there? 15
The secrets of my prison house 18
Speak within door 20
Melancholy sits on brood 23
Nothing but ourselves 25
One that was a woman, sir 26
I have a daughter (have while she is mine) 28
Let in the maid 30
In the middle of her favors 32
Bounded 34
The owl was a baker's daughter 35
Country matters 37
Your sister's drowned 38
Sweets to the sweet 39
Buried quick with her, and so will I 40
Sparrows 42
A chorus, my lord 44
Take up the bodies 46
We will bestow ourselves 47
Like the paintings of a sorrow 49
A document in madness 51
To this favor she must come 53
A green girl 55

a green boy

The trappings and the suits 59
This plague for thy dowry 60
The rest is silence 62
Of bell and burial 64

His way without his eyes	66
Of late . . . many tenders	68
For this relief	70
Against the burning	72
He weeps for what is done	74
'Tis not alone my inky cloak	76
They bleed on both sides	77
It started like a guilty thing	78
This pearl is thine	80
But if the water come to him	82

Jane Doe

A divided duty	87
I will play the swan	89
Death is our physician	91
Happiness to their sheets	93
Bells in your parlors	95
Entreat her to splinter	99
It strikes where it doth love	102

Acknowledgments	104

Author's Note

I first read *Hamlet* during my senior year in high school. I still have the essay I wrote hastily the night before & the morning it was due. "Although Hamlet eventually learns how to 'let be' and live," my thesis read, "he first learns that only by indirection is the truth found out, innocence gets raped, and man can never be at peace." What is now striking to me about my thesis & the writing that followed is that the focus was entirely on Hamlet. I hardly mentioned Ophelia, the *green girl*, who resonates with me the most.

The reason I initially overlooked her may be that Ophelia is often viewed as a one-dimensional character. She is depicted through the lens of mostly male characters who direct her narrative. She's not assigned a past or a personality & is apparently only desirable to Hamlet because of her physical beauty. No explanation is given for her missing mother, & Ophelia is nothing if not submissive. Only through her madness does she find her voice—that voice being a way for her to survive. But no one understands it or even tries to.

Ophelia is very much like the water she drowns in: she takes the shape of whatever contains her, & it's the men in her life who do that—Polonius, Laertes, Claudius, Hamlet. When Ophelia breaks into seemingly nonsensical song, dispenses imaginary flowers, & summons an imaginary coach, she finally starts to draw her own shape.

This, however, is a Catch-22. When she is sane, she is

suppressed & told what to do. When she is perceived as insane, she is balked at, misunderstood, her reality denied. In the end, she "turns to favor and to prettiness" & dies Narcissus-like, pulled down by an image of herself—that of the girl others wanted her to be. She disappears—water mixing with water.

My older sister, Jenny, was a green girl. Like Ophelia, she was beautiful (which is its own particular & insidious container); like Ophelia, her world became directed by other people. Jenny was sexually abused at a young age, raped when she was older. She spent most of her life addicted to drugs & alcohol, anorexic & bulimic; she was also my best friend, my closest ally, the only person I have known who understood me as I understand myself. At thirty-two, she died in a bathtub after a seizure—her eyes yellow, her body bony & bruise-spattered. Not long before she died, my ever-brave & loving sister gave me permission to share her story with others. She hoped it might help them avoid what she could not.

I, too, am a green girl. Like my sister, I was also sexually abused; then, as a teenager, groomed into further abuse by much older men. From childhood to early adulthood, I could not find the language to describe or come to terms with it. With no real understanding of what was done to me, I kept silent & instead scoured my world for any outlet that would somehow translate the loud, ever-tangling knot in my head into something more tolerable. I had no illusions it would go away.

In high school, I played basketball until my ankles blistered & bled. I'd dive for the ball like a raging rag doll hoping to quiet & subdue that knot. It is no surprise that I was also a cutter; the secret of it, hidden under long sleeves during the off-season or scar-friendly knee socks, was part of the attempt at translation.

So was writing. I feverishly penned parts of poems on arms, napkins, textbooks, notebooks—any surface would do, especially in the middle of the night.

Years before I started writing these poems, I knew I wanted to weave together my words with Shakespeare's & my story with Jenny's & Ophelia's. During the actual writing, however, I experienced a new trauma more debilitating than all others that preceded it. What now feels like a long way into this, I connected with Emilia from *Othello*; throughout most of the play, she is naively submissive to Iago who she trusts & obeys, but when she finally understands the absolute monster he is, she doesn't hold back on telling the truth, despite the risk that raising her voice puts her in. Before Iago kills her, she speaks "as liberal as the north" on behalf of another green girl, Desdemona.

The difference between her voice & Ophelia's? When Emilia speaks, she is actually listened to & understood.

Here's something about being green, at least in my experience: those who abuse that color & prey on it depend on our silence. They use it against us.

Polonius calls his daughter Ophelia a green girl to diminish her, to quiet her, to make her think of herself as helplessly naïve, dependent, & weak. He strips away her sense of self & then, like others, he uses her. As I wrote these poems, I wanted to change the green girl's narrative: not to do the impossible & change what has happened, but to *show* the secret parts. I believe every time we speak these difficult truths, rather than shame or silence them, we help give support to the resilience & strength that a green girl has; & those who listen can be a fulcrum to her survival.

 I have not discovered a happy ending or a silver lining in being a green girl—but contributing to her voice & shape has been a start.

 All of the poem titles & most of the italicized lines in this book are from Shakespeare's *Hamlet* & *Othello*.

green girls

Who's there?

I.
It was a girl
on her favorite swing, her aerial ballet

performed over birch stumps
& wish-flowers, where nettle beds

carpeted the tundra, where peonies
& columbine hummed

their afternoon sonata
of butterflies & bees

beneath umbrella clouds, the summer sky
like a bluebell, the girl's baggy overalls

with many pockets
for wild raspberry & pinecone

pebbles from neighbors' driveways
or where hiking trails broke into the river

dirt wedged in every toenail, her unbrushed hair
soaked by the backyard sprinkler—

she never had to ask
if there's safety in numbers.

II.
Before the swing set rusted
before her spindly legs filled with muscle—

she brightened & smiled at you, that cunning man
she trusted, but *out of her own goodness*

you made *the net*
to *turn her virtue into pitch*

left the wrinkle
stuck low in her throat

which kept the words
from coming up.

III.
She bends over a fog-wet pond
dry-heaves vertigo & scarp

in the clotted streamlet
where other girls have dropped

with no melee their seeds
like smashed kumquats

or tomatoes blistered
hot in the dark.

　　　　　By now it's too late, & you will never
　　　　　stand and unfold yourself

　　　　　try to change what's left
　　　　　of her fate—

she will borrow
her own heart

& let the water lick
the battered screen

the turning doorknob
until she plummets

like a sulking fruit, an organ
bloated soft in the sink

then

she will be her own sentinel
long after this happens

to scour your rust
from the swing.

The secrets of my prison house

I.
A bruised plum knows its own wound
keeps it secret in plain view

the center never the same
its fountainhead changing.

Bite into inviting skin
spongy flesh recoils the tongue

no remedy for a trauma
that cannot be undone.

II.

When you picked me, it was
my bruises that caught your eye—

back then, all my injuries
were salient to a passerby

no disguise against
what I could not see:

things rank and gross in nature.
You took me   to a grocery store

kneaded apricots
as if you had done it before

chose the blush-tinged
with velvet fuzz, just the right give.

When your teeth sunk hard
into the first one—how firm & sweet

I was   until you left me
its stony kernel

a prison house
for the seed.

Speak within door
for Audrey & Daisy

I.
Two girls baited
to separate parties

felt safe before
what happened started

(the prelude's always the same):
those boys were only playing

with aphids in a bug jar
that dashed from end to end

then   mouth-first into
a drunken villanelle

the refrains overtly violent—

he didn't slough off a wing
or a leg, though

he split the heart-part
of her torso

    so she could *make*
    no more noise with it

at the time.

II.
Didn't they know better
than to get into

that jar
in the first place

is what the whole town said
loud as every bellwether

who leaves the top untwisted, just so,
trapping *a song of willow*

she could not unhear.
Warm & pretty, peaty innards

turned sharp as hangnails—
the girls are dead.

One was like a hedgehog,
her brother said

she kept her outline
ever-barbed, needlelike

after the forced quilling
of her child spines—

always heard her *suitors following*
but would *not look behind.*

Melancholy sits on brood

Because *madness in* green *ones*
must not unwatched go

he gently knocked without reply
while my car was parked below

then hung a tote full of cereal
on the doorknob that fall.

I waited ten years to let him know
I was home after all

arched over like a fetus
bleaching wine from the sink

my fingers sore & tacky
my hair in clammy strings.

I pulled up wet threads
from a rug spot

one by one
pressed them into a quiet lump

of *thunders in the index*
& *incestuous sheets*—

        whatever was unspoken
        was already interred.

While other visitors had all
been ignored

I tempered my breath
when I heard him at the door.

Much is still the same
like an egg

that won't break
the center no longer warm

its mother broods
in the other place.

Nothing but ourselves

Along blue confetti walls of our ward
patients loop cold hallways
horseshoe-like & bright.

Who is the one always breaking free
from the guarded line?　　*Speak to me*—
pigtailed, legging-clad, glitter-eyed—

sometimes (all the time) I want her
to stay, here, in my bones
heavy where the silence lies

where what is hoarded is organized
in thy orisons

like a glass-green row of earthy wines
emptied in their prime.

The girl isn't me, or you, or some fiction—
she is the *before*: jaunty & spry
belly-cramped with laughter—

you & I
knotted and combined
are merely　　the *after*.

One that was a woman, sir
for Dr. Blasey Ford

I.
During the maelstrom
I was a gob of clay
laughed at wildly

shaped into a crude facsimile
by your drunken, vile hands.

You never finished—was that mercy?
Like a custard that will not set
my self-portrait now a vignette—

I dog-eared the page until it was
my landscape,
all else a canyon of blur—

      didn't you know
           epinephrine seals the denouement.

II.
She recovers her voice
before we stop to listen—

it spreads like a braided river—glacial, jarring,
her story *indelible in the hippocampus*

for us   & among the suited men
who cover her mouth again

sweep brave women
to the quiet ends.

III.
Take a spotlight to that hidden place
where the before-girls all incubate

& their imposters outlive them—
walk the ruined landscape to understand

how he undid her, then
step between her and her fighting soul

be a meta-voyeur of her mirror.

I have a daughter (have while she is mine)

I.
In the room with two sister beds, one sister
left. The other, a slow die-er,
like a bright boiling frog
tired of aligning to its princess—

wafer-thin in her winter
she cut her lip on the Cheval glass
I gave her

being too close to the mirror
that's privy to her beauty
& her wiles.

II.
I forbade her to leave that night
tore down posters & photos

yelled louder than
her dizzy lies.

There was a pause—
her gaunt, pale legs took anchor
moonlight burned into the glossy pane.

Divided from herself
she pushed up the window
leaned forward
disconsolate & wild—

III.
Go back.
All my father-words: placebo

if I could still hold you
while you kick & scratch
until police arrive

there were endless other windows
I would wait beside.

In your eyes still dwell the endnotes
I'll never read, never edit—

>once I tossed away a tomato
>for its white, moldy spine

>you scolded me
>said to ignore the damaged part
>with a chopping knife—

>but after the incision
>the other side is realized

>& never leaves you.

Let in the maid

There are more open graves than beds
for those we could rescue from disrepair

so tell my sister, who has stumbled
from elsewhere to nowhere

inside nightmare-polyped years
that you were there as well

tired of every sunset
every melting nameless star

no one a witness
as you ghosted along the crescent-edge

of a whiskey-slicked drain-hole
sinking into the mattress mold.

Tell her it was never as lovely as it was
when nascent, when the first drink

ribboned inward its blushing gift—
how soon it became recurrence & fetor

no longer the warm ease & calm
to apron the loathing you lived on.

Tell her any secret she keeps
you already know—

if she has ever let a stranger rearrange her
for a drug, used lab scalpels & shaving blades

to carve herself a visible heart
with brimming chambers, red severed loaves—

if she's ever hidden money from herself
beneath feathered pillows

or felt her children extraneous,
mothering them a tedious chore.

Tell her it's not her fault, & she isn't alone—
that neither of you

has to be anchored,
wasted, possessed

tell her she is home.

In the middle of her favors

I.
I never make love
to him, not any of them

on my childhood roof
gritty shingles scratch

long purples across my lower back
harrow night into my eyes

until the stars bend
to hold me as he climbs—

>*we'll teach you*
>*to drink deep*
>*ere you depart*

suspended dweller, you think *his will*
is not his own—

>now, relent this
>& this forever.

II.
He thinks I am shy, knows I am ill—
a drunken novice   spread like a fledgling

on sodden leaves
the trees litter

my begging call
more like a wheeze

lingers after
the nectar is swilled.

III.
Bourbon down the drain
where my favors ebb & tether

you've looked but not seen
these dark jewels I've gathered
to paint a spring green—

trace each with your finger
like a scar I carve & enter

as *the unweeded garden
grows to seed.*

Bounded

My eye at the peephole
has begun to itch   this is same old same old:

bookshelves & closets full
the kitchen fat—

here's a vat of milk & whiskey
you'll make warm
when our bodies heap

but don't touch me
when I'm looking

let me trawl the relic-bloated halls
of pickled memory

let me near the fissure
of the door with no key—

        a sparrow smacks into the window
        trying to get in   or kiss its twin
        her broken throat now part of our debris.

You keep her here
to *color your loneliness*

all our mirrors
are apologies.

The owl was a baker's daughter

Smile or hide when the bell chimes
I am not myself if you enter

play the game, don't believe it
was father's ill advice

but I am soft
& so I seek it—

when the dough that rises
gets over-kneaded, you take me

as I have been taken twice
before, stiff as a day-old loaf

stacked on the baker's sill—*let it be
tenable in your silence still*

but what's done isn't always ready
& I'm no one else's girl—

look you now what follows:

my talons sharp & hungry

for what's no longer
fresh—plain as a well-used doll

it's the changing
that I envy.

Country matters

My thighs open
like a birthday present

summon you to a cherry
that's counterfeit—

as *thou com'st*
in such a questionable shape, I pretend

you are someone else
sing threnodies for the dead

       nothing's enough—

bite into my own hand, *a toy in blood*
until I can't feel you pillage

can't feel
when you're done—

don't call it sacrifice
       I do this every time

don't towel off the lees
       relinquish them to me.

Your sister's drowned
for Jenny

Rum in your old cup is an empty mirror
no face nearby to color my memory—

seven long years, your absence
a famine

all the doors to return to you
another ocean's timber

too much of water hast thou—

you passed in a bathtub
not the traditional way

your head still crowned
above the watery grave

what you abandoned
made your slim body seize
your tongue sever

the doctor said, *do not drink*
& you agreed, forever.

Sweets to the sweet

No one's invited to dine
in this room—I pile-high
another bowl, promise it's the last—

I am hungry in the place
that's never full.

Each cherry spreads hives
& plants a bony seed

split from black-violet suits
that burn my tongue
& plug my teeth.

If by the dim-lit mirror
you slink & spy

*never make known
what you have seen tonight:*

I'll wash the clotted dye
& bury the stems

between us
where there needs no ghost.

Buried quick with her, and so will I

In a chamber far from here
charred to flakes of bone
all the soft parts gone

like aurora pulled from winter sky
her dancing neon   now a dull, sickly knoll

the you that's left behind
this cylinder of cinders

bubble-wrapped in a box—
the default container.

Our postman cannot know
the woman he delivers

        where are your brown eyes
        I envied for their cellars
        the moss & mildew you made bright

        your raven-straight hair
        drifting out the car window

        or the tawny birthmark
        on your left thigh
        now a fiery tendril.

For my portion, a silver urn
that's for remembrance

a pink one for your daughter
who asked what the ashes felt like

        (a fine sand on my palm)

the rest to mom & dad
who keep you on a shelf

to what base uses
we may return

the sum of your hundred pounds
reduced to three & divvied out.

Sparrows

>   *for Jenny, for Abby*

I.
My sparrow never met
a sky that wasn't glass

or a mirror that did not
show her coming nearer

her pretty wings flicked
downward in a vodka bath

her tongue like a stone, ever-
loud, with song to scare

all who dared come close—
she wore her doom

like a *sea-gown*
all tuft & rib

starved her little bones
in the furrow where she lived.

II.
Your sparrow
lost her polestar

dove vein-first
into that halcyon

river, took the shape
of its languid bed—

took from your eye its opus
your downy wing, *this changeling*

never known
though your likeness

& hers
not entirely gone—

you left copies of yourselves   behind
as green girls often do—

        daughters loved from the grave
        still always start out blue.

A chorus, my lord

In the center of the loudest room
I wait for you in white

sneakers, tight high-pony,
plaid sleeves to cover blood graffiti—

I am sixteen, you are fifty & in charge
of me, insist I'm an old soul

at 2 a.m., our nightly phone call—
you send me *Late Night Thoughts on Listening*

to Mahler's Ninth Symphony
& a strappy mini dress in taupe

for August, the bland hotel, corner suite
I knock three times, do not linger—

on the wall, a neon sign
for celebrating

on the table, a bowl of ice
for nipples & kissing

on the bed, your rough hands
part my ankles, pump between my thighs—

this is when, *by indirections*,
my body borrowed & flaccid

I paint a sky that's free of you
blurry & bird-calm, my eyes shut

where I'm still folded
a wet concertina

gone are the girly pieces.

Take up the bodies

To you that look pale
wilted & dragging

through sticky mycelial cells,
when this hive broods dim

& gutters debris
I *make a ghost of him*

that lets me
turn from woman

to child
to undertaker—

can't meet my own eyes
in this mirror—I'm no queen

but I know better
how to hunger-strike the honey

that once coated my lips
spurn your right to touch

in the walls where I live
like a glass that leaves

no watermark—
even bees rake out their dead.

We will bestow ourselves

At fourteen, the looking glass saw
my body pistil-thin & blurred

from bath steam, my likeness
with *an antic disposition on*

& the dark widow's peak
like a nomad that would not leave

emerged
to obscure what was left.

I was one grim thing
so shaved *away the worser part*

until my face was strange
then stranger.

> *If, like a crab,*
> *I could go backward—*

but I did not know then
none of my graves
is accidental

& that room at fourteen
is this room, too

where the mirrors are labyrinths
can't tell who's who.

Like the paintings of a sorrow

Let us not *impart*
what we have seen tonight

but wake icky & sore
already divided —

>   if one of us leaves,
>   the other must endure.

Long stayed he so
when I was dizzy drunk

left us to scald
the blood-rill

& plummy patches—
hot water on thigh-skin

like a pot of milk that wrinkles
black on the stove

no use peeling its film off—
this isn't injury, we know

>   *suit the action to the word:*
>   what's nameless isn't real—

she leaves the room & the body
I grit my teeth & stay—

which isn't treason
it's mimesis

either way
you can't see us

nor which one draws the razor
or the bath.

A document in madness

My unsleeved arms, indelible
with angry scars

that shrivel white when cold
& bloom purple in the sun—

words I never meant
to speak

save on my periphery—
full disclosure

is accidental honesty—
at thirteen, I ran

a kitchen knife
hard across my wrist

marveled at the scarlet ribbon
sparkling & vivid—

gashes were heavy & quick
their shiny mouths surprised & slow to drip

burns were long & yawning, a last resort
for my impatience—

my now-faded injuries
like *weedy trophies*

       for what I've abandoned
       I also possess—

the cross-hatch on my thigh
the sight word on my ankle:

die. A portrait, a painting,
the blood set free long gone—

all I wanted out
that still simmers inside

but what's visible—
this jagged mural   is mine.

To this favor she must come

Low on secrets, I found a nest
like a temple on the ground

near budding strawberries, four eggs
speckled with beige & mosquitoes.

Her wings warm & threadbare,
the mother bird went away.

I watched her unborn for days—
when the sky was gypsum-white,

the grass like a thicket,
one began to hatch—a chick

her head wobbly, not yet with song—
I lay down beside her

saw her pink skin & blackened eyes.
The next morning, my father

backed his trailer across the egg spot,
the girl paper-flat, without a cry,

 just a glazed line of blood.
Their mother came.

Hopped across the wet streak,
breakfast dangling in her mouth—

until summer's end she returned where
all the eyes were blotted out

& I misunderstood then
why she purled where her dead lie—

her doleful dance was not penitence
but a plea: here, *may violets spring*.

A green girl

is not afraid to die
not quite

soon she'll join the others
who are fettered

to that far country
where birds are small & never scream.

A green girl lets
her fingers pierce the bad plum

with asylum
that warm seeping center

as though she touches her own insides
to draw apart the body

& leave the bones
that hold her stick-shape—

the offal & shiny braids
to cover up what's left behind.

A green girl knows
her own crime scene

does all the tedious work—
the writing & the dusting

for the ones who've kept her like a bird
stuck in the kitchen vent

its mad-flapping wings & chirps
lost in the interstice.

A green girl *turns*
to favor and to prettiness

with blue & yellow garlands, bronzy eyes,
pearly cheeks & rose-lacquered lips—

& still, the child who looks back
is ill & does not fit.

Below the water
is the mud-pack

for the tired & the reticent
whose thighs have kept their bruises

& for those who might die sober
but will never be blue—

>   I'm a green girl,
>   are you?

a green boy

The trappings and the suits

I shall obey & molt
without him, sleep between the instars.

I eat my own shed skin
when the mulberry's gone

naked, tight, horned
not fit for his queen—

>in the wanton harvest I imagine
>under satin, slaking sheets

>he unravels the dark things
>from my full belly, not me.

My wintry home, where the ceiling
is also the floor, protects me: *best safety lies in fear*

but these sticky figure 8s I weave from my mouth
limber loud with *words, words, words*   I used to bury.

When my last silk thread spins the lattice
when all the poems are out, I ready my dowry—

not for his *hot love on the wing*
our moth bodies supple & cloying

but for the boiling.

This plague for thy dowry

In your green garden, one of us outlives
the other—forbidden to love, to writhe

glassy-warm, feral, teeming
between sentinel weeds —

*there is a kind of confession
in your looks,* & I am never the same girl twice

spied from the dark side
of a half-silvered mirror.

They think us mad—we *eat the air,
promise-crammed*, stifled when we scream.

Neither daughter nor woman, I stay where I am
& you, my stinging tree

root just close enough, but not to touch
or be touched—

hungry for the fruit you bear
its inky gift pumped

through saw-tooth leaves
venom-tipped hairs—

when I taste you
the fever is my own

I give it a name, take it home
put its fire *into a dew*—

the bathwater brimming
over, soon.

The rest is silence

I.
I poured out the whiskey
with the man who kept me

like a seedy heirloom, or a thing
hung crooked on the wall—

his feral, booming voice
that shook metal hinges

is gone—now I'm alone
my pigeon ribs stick out

as I scour the house
launder the hoary squalor

he left in my bed
tear in half every picture

of a girl who wasn't there
& gave her *thoughts no tongue.*

II.
All the outsides & edges
twice-bleached, wiped clean

& what was guarded is now
unearthed to you

a green boy who *sees*
the inmost part

with eyes like calm sea ice
that cut through mine

until it hurts   just right
& I read to you

an inky chorus
here, where curtains are drawn

where words in shallow graves
never stay too long.

Of bell and burial

My other half, a temptress in repose,
appears bare-skinned & longing

where *nothing's either good or bad*
but thinking makes it so—

no longer new
yet like a hungry novice

I cannot bridle her
or put her on mute—

here she is, on her knees
a smitten ghost:

wants you like a dark that drowns
when the power's out

wants your chest & mouth
all the inches of you
to soften & harden—

that's a lonely freedom
dark sky with no stars

when she isn't even

allowed you
without *quiet pass*—

our body wintry, unused
the *bride-bed* bloody

when she's removed.

His way without his eyes

I meet your lower lip
where your sorrow's spent

feel a pallid scar
that's a blueprint on your wrist

the mark of a boy
who sought *his quietus*
in peril & madness.

When our fingers touch
our hiding places—

flesh that built dams
where we bled –

we idle there
grapes without skins

the fruit bedewed
their centers full —

I know how you feel
never has to be said

silent where we're warm
& coalesce—

I don't have permission
that's true

but you're the only mirror
I look into.

Of late . . . many tenders

When moonlight burns on my bed
I taste the scar that's buried in your lip

your chest heaving, sea-heavy
under sheets that peal in waves

our bodies warm & searching—
your palm, where the dull knife sank in

presses hard on my breast
apple-pink with gooseflesh

from the cold that sticks
rigid at the window & wants in . . .

Be you & I behind an arras then

outside, the winter solstice
stows the sun back in her cellophane

while here in our secret place
you fit just right inside me

& don't mind the girl who's kept there
her eyes too young for watching.

In the shower, soap suds pepper us
like pearls & disappear—

we move glassy-wet in prosody,
words disinterred from a long-quiet film

now stressed & unstressed
in battalions, in tumid ebbs

that *draw you into madness*
& make our blood new again.

For this relief

I.
Cicadas stirred the summer nights
in the hot south where I was raised

with a shrill, drum-like call
that would frighten me awake.

One night I heard a wingless nymph
split open her back to shed her frame

on the large oak tree I used to climb
to get farther & further away.

I found something strange
stuck on the bark—

a brittle wraith left on pause
once the adult, fresh & wet

emerged in the liquid dark
& had to be brave. I envied her

       future offspring
       who'd burrow under the rich,

       rooted soil   until at least
       the age of seventeen

& with shame, I crunched the carapace
into crumbs beneath my feet.

II.
When you finally take me
our bellies full of sex

& glazed with sweat
your green-gray eyes soft & spent

my hair in tendrils
on your beating neck—

it is long after this
the ghastly shell picked off my toes

& my own guarded casing, zipped down
like a dress & left on your floor—

whenever I'm with you,
I'm new

& *assume a pleasing shape.*

Against the burning

For us to live with our dead—
those *forty thousand brothers*

who took their time,
took our young, green meat

from the olive pit—
we live with the living

in a candlelit lair, join
like water beads on an icy glass

your body plumed & rigid, my eyes
riled & gilded   remind you

that not having you
felt like this:

as if my son
still rooted for my breast

the milk-knot that burns
& billows up

ready to drain
inside his parted lips

& you take him, just before
the hard, wet latch

my love unspent & scalding.
Now, with my teeth

I drink wine from your neck
sink wanton nails into your sodden back

so deep my glitter polish chips
& sticks to your salt-blood skin—

this is it, the nucleus,
your soul knows my soul

& I claim you, green boy.

He weeps for what is done

My green boy's inhuman
in his private mirror

his eyes stupid-sad
his frame thinner.

The noise in his head
is also my own

I bleed where he is cut
& disappear when he's alone.

My green boy is dark
in his bed—

would choke me
with his right hand

stop my breath
with his left.

It was happiness
to blindfold my eyes

& tie with rope
my ankles & wrists.

Now he is all pallor & self-torment
says *get thee* to a different therapist.

He's washed me off the sheets
& returned my gifts

sees only the base monster
I have made of him

but he's more like the book
he gave me before we kissed:

Love's Executioner. Green boy. Soulmate.
Our *madness shall be paid with weight.*

'Tis not alone my inky cloak

We were a dark & lovely secret
wreathed to each like seaweed

twisting until we severed, our wild cadence
unrelenting   now stopped.

The last meal we shared sits
rotting in my fridge

the gloomy office where we met
the green house where we might have lived

from plenum to vacuum
neither will be filled with us.

All week I have eaten like an ill bird
& at night, stand half-dressed in the frigid wind

that it might eddy me up to erase me —
if this is what you want.

I made my wrist puff out hard on one side
so it purples & strangles the scars you touched

but nothing will absolve—no penitence
belongs to us. My wet & nettled eyes

forever with thy vailed lids   *seek* for you
to seal them shut.

They bleed on both sides

Our green garden's overgrown & loamy
the flowers bald, their slighted petals splintered off

& the once-wild silken lilies
now a sun-bleached stale tissue—

our provenance is a tainted story we relate
in heaping detail to a stranger each week

that love is merely madness, its welting ache
runs through us   carnal, sieve-like.

Things standing thus unknown
I build the gallows at your door

our poems in their ill-fated order
our eyes both startled & rusted over—

I can no longer ask you
to lick the blood from my side

The foul practice hath turned itself on me—
already marred where it mattered,

I rehearse your words & hoard my grief
so its *millions of acres* become my tomb—

unless *Hamlet from himself be ta'en away*
you still have the egg tooth.   It's you.

It started like a guilty thing

I.
When you were a child
the ice-haired huskies
tried to keep you safe

until they slept, rescue-drunk & frigid-eared
your small body curled in theirs—

but the neighbor boys
with sordid mouths & hands
became your carolers of pain to bear

the flesh at first a red thread
bloomed open
despite *the very armor* you *had.*

Of that infinite trespass
you & I are sapient—
know the *prologue to the omen coming on.*

II.
The blue clock keeps falling
from my kitchen wall

its broken anthem jarring
then rhythmic as a faucet drip.

I've stopped the filmy tedium
of chores & eating meals

since our distancing
preserved in some isometry

I mistook as anchor
for the sorrow we had earned.

Now I'm your tongueless semaphore
waving frantically these poems to you
& *green*, our safe word.

This pearl is thine

I met you in the healing place—

all my mantles tightly heaped
were yours to strip & mine to ink

but *what a falling off was there*

the trauma that we shared
compelled us to repeat it &

   consent

to pull the sternum from my chest
climb my ribs like ladder rungs

squeeze each chamber with your trusted hand
& pump your wounded blood in

whither wilt thou lead:
to release or reinjure

the latter *sets a* branded *blister there*
that fills but does not weep—

thought-sick at the bedroom *act*, you confessed
& left me in the nunnery scene

all our mantles tightly heaped, plus
our *union* in this cup
that's my sacrifice to drink—

there will be no more parts   when you
& I   & our bad actors meet
in the same dust.

But if the water come to him

I.
Others, too, know the center seam
is where cicatrix hides the hemorrhage

where we formed a new language:

I am to you
as thou art to thyself

&

"you would look so fuckable
in a collar."

Beneath my skin-tight white-heart-printed romper
was black lace &   somewhere, a woman

limbs twisted back   the face blocked out
with blindfold & gag ball

red handprints where you pulled
the reins of my hips

for the last time—   *I have no life to breathe*
what thou hast done, counselor,

but on your black car's winter-dirtied glass
with my finger, I smeared:

>he binds her
>to him
>then makes her
>disappear.

II.
If these poems
are a bird's eye view

to the body I gave
that wasn't mine to give

& like water, had no shape
until you contained it—

then *bend your eye on vacancy*

for those that follow
are *as liberal as the north*—

a nimbus, bearing rain.

Jane Doe

A divided duty

The place where it started—a turning point,
to put it mildly—isn't mine to make a shelter in

I'm told   the entire center is like a field
that will fallow if I enter.

Now in double-exile   I start to wonder
how I can still love   what I should hate, except

I am not what I am

arms & legs crudely sutured like mismatched socks
seepage pooling in the furrow—

the constant static   of something else's grim memories
kept behind lidless eyes   so I'll not sleep tonight.

I scrub with vinegar the veiny tapestry
until it's hot & harlot-red.   Listen—

I am not what I am

all day I've been
playing house with a stranger

a reverse blur of nose, cheek, hair
a rumor, a fracture, a slattern   who asked for it

on the leather couch, where the mark I left—
a green inkblot—even that's not there.

I am not what I am

this bleating, antic figment
strangles the flower necks   to frolic with the dead, smiles

when the scissors in its hand
appear in mine instead

says *the bruised heart* must be *pierced through the ear*—
take the blade & find your shelter there.

I will play the swan

There's a secret   kept distal
in bath-warm tears I muffle

just here   in my full-length mirror
that's always   never right.

What's me
that wasn't you

when the original   taken out
looks slanted, rippled   grim as

the last words you wrote: Return
to Sender.

Spring meltwater
bathes the pondweeds

in a late-dripping sun.
Someone's about to find

where the bodies lie—
like scabbed pecans
dropped from their branches.

With what violence
you *first loved* me—

in this selfsame pool
the nests reamed   & feather-full.

Death is our physician

I only really knew you
in the winter—

it's nearly fall—storm-birthed leaves
pool a soggy ochre

that cataracts
across this clammy deck

the grass below cloud-cold, bent
the last sweet tomatoes

pink-green, belly-split
hang like doll parts

over squash flowers
that prickle my hardened skin.

How many times you walked up
the ice-banked stairs—

after, I dashed your footprints
too fancy for the snow that gathered there.

If it were now to die—
not like a season that's passed

or the once-manic anthill
its cadent bowels washed out its side

but how we might
throw out our eyes

to console them
& *steal away, so guilty-like.*

Happiness to their sheets

I didn't even know his eyes
were green, not blue, or that he swore

an oath to do no harm
to those who wanted rescue.

        He said, "I always feel like I'm looming
        over you," then moved

where I sat tight & shaking
my ankle socks flat on the wooden floor

lamplit with each ill memory
I leaked.

The beginning was rehearsal—
my mouth a bloody plum

so I would not tell
what ended sour & lumped—

he tied me naked
to his ceiling beam

mused out loud
a stranger rape scene

& swatted hard with his hand
my slight curves

that still
bristle pink & break—

        I am not where
        I'm supposed to be.

If *the robbed that smiles*
steals something from the thief

I'm the sharp
& bony sequel

scratching at the lid
that keeps him.

Bells in your parlors

I.
I slept in & stayed
in the house you rented up the icy

switchback, just for the day—
sipped black coffee under hanging paper lanterns

bit into a crisp Fuji apple
the size of my cupped hand   then, I confess,

I turned into a sleuth when I saw
our still-soft blindfold not far

from a similar one
coated with dust & someone else's hair.

I stretched it taut in front of my eyes
& felt a peel

rise & stick behind my tongue,
acidic before it went back down—

a white shoebox centered
as if the books were its audience

where you kept inside Mary's
cards & letters, her careful cursive notes

& trinkets—she loved you, I'm sure,
even after all her words belonged not in the air

but in there.
I inched across the room as though you were still close,

watching   (I am heel-heavy
& stomp even when I am walking).

In your bedside drawer, a pair
of black latex gloves

& a small envelope I'd inked
with my name & yours—

I smeared your favorite minty Chapstick
on my lips, to taste you,

found other pairs of gloves
in the bathroom, living room,

& on the Welcome mat outside
by a blue broom

where I tucked your keys
under the worn bristles.

II.
For seven weeks, my body was
your nighttime toy,

fun & bendy
my head like glass

a slow ballad
that was breaking.

You moved out
long after my car's snowy dent

from the spinning wheel
on the curve-steep drive   melted

not quite like my backside
that stung hot pink & welted

from your hand that once helped me
up the high wooden bed.

What art thou?   Can you still see me
on our last night, Valentine's,

blinded, gagged, patiently
hogtied—

every single thing you did
was surfeit

a recurring scene
in a play with one purpose:

> *the purchase made,*
> *the fruits are to ensue.*

When you handed me the spatula
to sweep bell peppers

into a sizzling pan, I felt inside
a hardening statue

& since then, every meal I'd cooked for us
now tastes of sour-leather-sex—

I go somewhere else
when it all combines:

the boozy dark.
I try

to keep from you
what once I thought was mine.

Entreat her to splinter

I.
Rain beads on the far plant, a tiny ballroom
where each light sticks wet to the rim

& sputters up
quick, percussive.

One leaf distends
its belly, gets seeded
by the parasitic
oak gall wasp—

this dome now my nursery

will *silence* the *dreadful bell*
that *frights the isle*
to let me grow.

But the crypt-keeper wasp
punctures in
to set the other egg

where it will feed for days
on me, his chiral twin—that's counter-

transference, that's a sort of
love, & I *deny thee nothing*

as we labor & puff, our wings
more like hands   never

coincide
when we touch.

II.
Despite your warning—"this will not be
a regular breakup"—

I begin to burrow us
an escape hatch

my head the first
to pierce with ease

the gall's crispy skin
until you stop me

the cut too small
for both of us to leave—

      so *for our hurts*, your*self*
      will be my *surgeon.*

I feel you dig pin-sharp
& trudge the pinkish gel
that was my eye

my head—your trespass—
still wedged like a cork
plugs the space you left.

Pilgrimed parasite,
it is only now I know

that death's unnatural   *that kills*
for loving me so.

It strikes where it doth love

I.
You stated twice
you did not hurt me

a green girl
now become a Jane Doe

then said you once loved me
for the dangers I had passed

& that I'd made progress—

my transference   toward you
gone away, somehow,

behind shiny rose heads
you snapped back with ease.

       I know now those prickly thorns
       against my skin
       were just your human teeth

       that dragged me into a cold weedy plot
       my new counselor can never reach.

II.
You must have thought my *speech is nothing*
& I, too, have heard myself

so low-pitched & weak
that I belong where

summer flies are in the shambles
& hollowed seeds

canker in their soil
long before the galling.

But my son & daughter need me
more than when

outside the green house
outside your office

I felt I could not live
so here's a promise:

my injuries are just a sport to you
but it is from there

that I write
& will speak truth into the public's ear.

Acknowledgments

Poems from this collection appeared in the following:

Seneca Review (spring 2019): One that was a woman, sir; I have a daughter (have while she is mine); Let in the maid; Your sister's drowned; Buried quick with her; and so will I; Sparrows

Dogwood (spring 2020): A divided duty

Oberon (2020): Death is our physician

About Jessie Sobey

Jessie Sobey received a B.A. in English from Hobart and William Smith Colleges & an M.F.A. in poetry from University of Montana, Missoula. She lives with her children & husband in Interior Alaska.